CONTENTS

WELCOME TO THE WORLD OF INFOGRAPHICS

Using icons, graphics and pictograms, infographics visualise data and information in a whole new way!

DISCOVER HOW MANY PASSENGERS THERE ARE FOR EVERY CAR IN THE WORLD

MEASURE THE WORLD'S LARGEST SUPERMARKET IN FOOTBALL PITCHES

SEE HOW MUCH FOOD IS THROWN AWAY EVERY SINGLE DAY

COMPARE THE HEIGHT OF THE WORLD'S TALLEST BUILDINGS

MORE AND MORE PEOPLE

Improvements in diet and health care over the last 100 years have meant that many people are living for longer and fewer are dying young. This has led to an explosion in the world's population.

HOW MUCH LAND?
As the world's population has increased, so the amount of land for each person has decreased.

1900
0.09 SQUARE KILOMETRES EACH

1950
0.06 SQ KM EACH

2010
0.02 SQ KM EACH

2050
0.016 SQ KM EACH

CITY VS COUNTRY
Since 1800, more and more people have moved from the country to large cities.

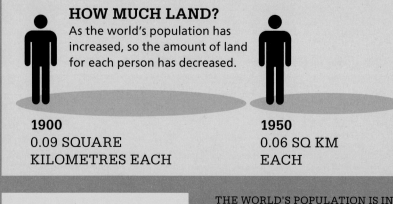

3% | 97%
1800

47% | 53%
2000

60% | 40%
2030

THE WORLD'S POPULATION IS INCREASING BY

74,000,000

EVERY SINGLE YEAR.

Double time

The time it has taken the world's population to grow by 1 billion has decreased. To grow from 2 billion to 3 billion took 32 years, but to grow from 5 billion to 6 billion took just 11 years.

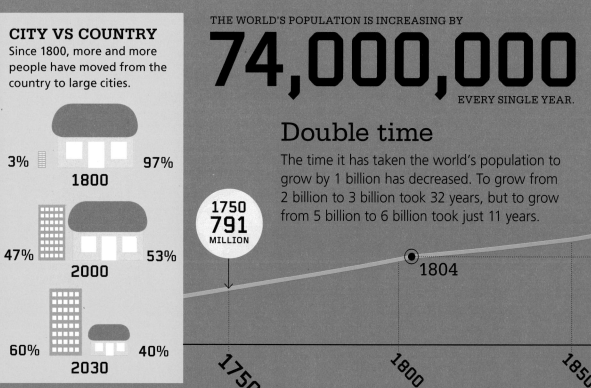

1750
791
MILLION

1804

1750

1800

1850

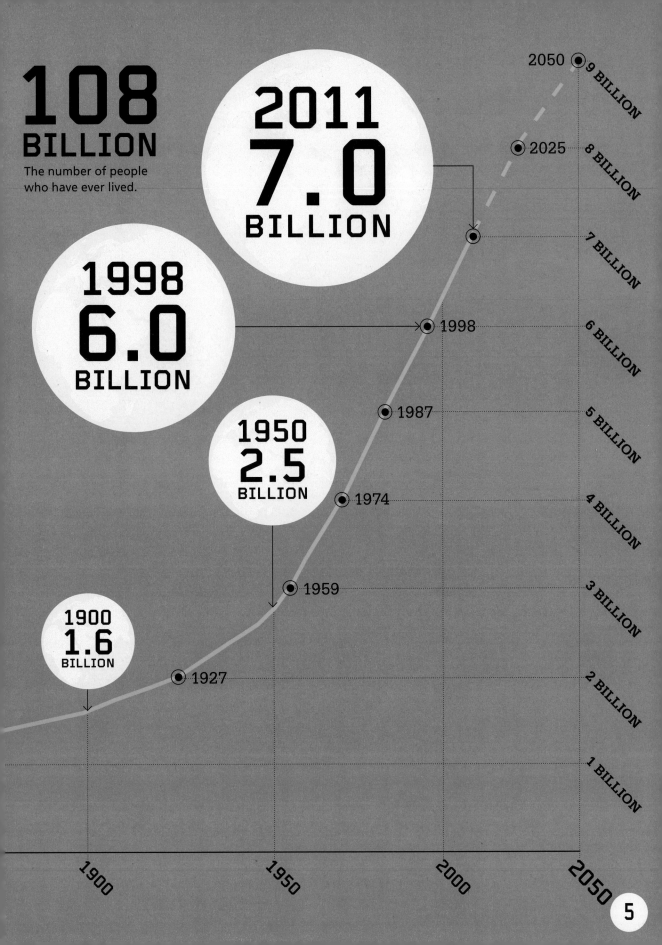

108 BILLION

The number of people who have ever lived.

2011
7.0 BILLION

1998
6.0 BILLION

1950
2.5 BILLION

1900
1.6 BILLION

2050 ● 9 BILLION

● 2025   8 BILLION

● 7 BILLION

● 1998   6 BILLION

● 1987   5 BILLION

● 1974   4 BILLION

● 1959   3 BILLION

● 1927   2 BILLION

1 BILLION

1900   1950   2000   2050

5

WHERE IN THE WORLD?

The distribution of the world's population is very uneven. While in some areas the average space each person has is the size of a small room, in others it can be the area of a town.

EUROPE
POPULATION
732,759,000
10.61%
OF WORLD POPULATION

GREENLAND
lowest population density in the world. Each person has 38.5 square kilometres.

NORTH AMERICA
POPULATION
351,659,000
5.09%
OF WORLD POPULATION

67
Population of the country with the fewest people – the Pitcairn Islands in the middle of the Pacific Ocean.

LATIN AMERICA AND THE CARIBBEAN
POPULATION
588,649,000
8.52%
OF WORLD POPULATION ···>

AFRICA
POPULATION
1,033,043,000
14.95%
OF WORLD POPULATION

ASIA

POPULATION

4,166,741,000

60.31%

OF WORLD POPULATION

MACAU, CHINA
highest population
density in the world.
Each person has
0.00005 square
kilometres.

1,336,720,000

Population of the People's Republic of China, the country with the most citizens.

OCEANIA
POPULATION
35,838,000
0.52%
OF WORLD
POPULATION

The ten countries
with the largest
number of people
account for 58.7
per cent of the
world's population.
The other countries
– nearly 200 – have
just 41.3%.

58.7%   41.3%

CITY LIVING

Towns and cities are found in nearly every part of the world, from mountain peaks to arid deserts. Some are so big, that more people live in them than in whole countries.

FIVE BIGGEST CITIES

The figures shown here represent the number of people found in each of these urban agglomerations. An agglomeration is a built-up area made up of the city and any suburbs that are linked to it.

2. DELHI
INDIA

22,157,000

Delhi is the largest agglomeration in terms of its area. Each person living here has an average space of 0.0015 square kilometres.

5. MEXICO CITY
MEXICO

19,460,000

Nine million people live in Mexico City, with the rest living in neighbouring areas.

3. SAO PAULO
BRAZIL

20,262,000

Covering an area of 8,000 sq km, Sao Paulo is the most populous city in the entire Americas.

4. MUMBAI
INDIA

20,041,000

Each person living in the agglomeration of Mumbai has an average of just 0.00006 square kilometres.

NORTHERNMOST AND SOUTHERNMOST SETTLEMENTS

The Canadian settlement of Alert lies just 817 km from the North Pole. At the other end of the Earth, Amundsen-Scott is a scientific base at the South Pole.

LA RINCONADA, PERU ·····>
5,099 M

Amundsen-Scott base
South Pole

Alert, Nunavut Canada

LA PAZ, BOLIVIA ·····>
3,640 M

CUZCO, PERU ·····>
3,300 M

1. TOKYO
JAPAN
36,669,000

The Greater Tokyo Area is the largest agglomeration in the world. It is so big that it has swallowed other cities entirely, including Yokohama, which has 3 million people on its own.

HIGHEST AND LOWEST

The settlement of La Rinconada is close to a gold mine high up in the Andes Mountains. Despite its remote location, 30,000 people live and work there.

DENVER, USA ·····>
1,609 M

In 1950, there were **83** cities with populations of more than **1 million** people. By **2007**, this had risen to **468**.

PARIS, FRANCE
35 METRES ·····>

SEA LEVEL

JERICHO, WEST BANK
APPROX 250 METRES ·····>
BELOW SEA LEVEL

REACH FOR THE SKY

Modern skyscrapers soar high into the air and are places where thousands of people live, work, shop and even relax in parks and swimming pools.

BURJ KHALIFA
The tallest building in the world contains:
160-ROOM HOTEL
11 HECTARES OF PARK
3,000 UNDERGROUND PARKING SPACES
26,000 PANES OF GLASS

The height of the world's first skyscraper, the Home Insurance Building built in Chicago in 1885.

42 M

The Great Pyramid of Giza in Egypt was the tallest building in the world from 2570 BCE until 1311 CE. It is made from approximately 2.3 million stone blocks and weighs about 5.75 million tonnes.

GREAT PYRAMID AT GIZA
147 M

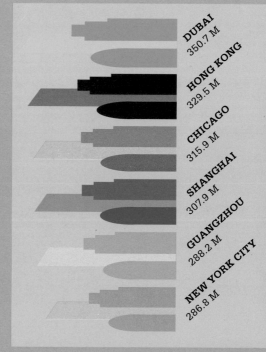

DUBAI
350.7 M

HONG KONG
329.5 M

CHICAGO
315.9 M

SHANGHAI
307.9 M

GUANGZHOU
288.2 M

NEW YORK CITY
286.8 M

TALLEST CITIES IN THE WORLD
These figures show the calculated average height of the ten tallest (CAHTT) buildings in each city. In 2010, Dubai became the world's tallest city when the Burj Khalifa was officially opened.

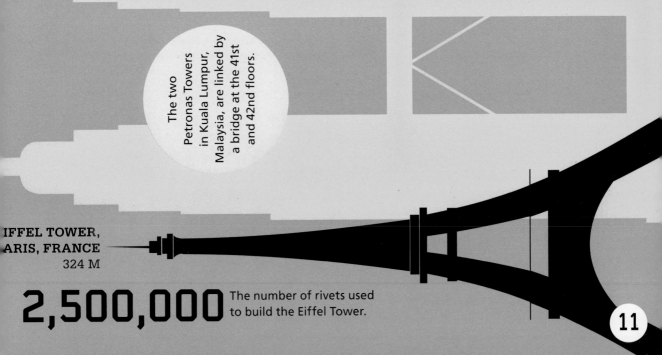

BURJ KHALIFA, DUBAI, UNITED ARAB EMIRATES 829.84 M

CN TOWER, TORONTO, CANADA 553.33 M

WILLIS TOWER, CHICAGO, USA 527 M

TAIPEI 101, TAIPEI, TAIWAN 509.2 M

PETRONAS TOWERS, KUALA LUMPUR, MALAYSIA 451.9 M

The two Petronas Towers in Kuala Lumpur, Malaysia, are linked by a bridge at the 41st and 42nd floors.

**IFFEL TOWER,
ARIS, FRANCE**
324 M

2,500,000 The number of rivets used to build the Eiffel Tower.

RICH WORLD, POOR WORLD

Trade spreads money and wealth around the world. But this wealth is not spread evenly – many people are very poor while some countries can afford to borrow enormous amounts of money.

WHERE ARE THE RICH?

This map shows the percentage of the world's wealth held by different areas around the globe.

NORTH AMERICA 28%

THE RICHEST 0.5% OF THE WORLD'S POPULATION OWN 38.5% OF ITS WEALTH THE POOREST TWO THIRDS OWN JUST 3.3%

SOUTH AMERICA **4%**

World trade

Countries need to buy in certain goods from other parts of the world – this is called importing. The graphics below show the countries that import the highest value of goods.

90% The amount of the world's trade that is carried around the globe by shipping.

USA 2,314,000,000,000

CHINA 1,743,000,000,000

Import levels 2011 (US$).

US$1.7 TRILLION

The amount the public debt of the USA increased by in 2010. It rose by US$1.9 trillion in 2009 and US$1 trillion in 2008.

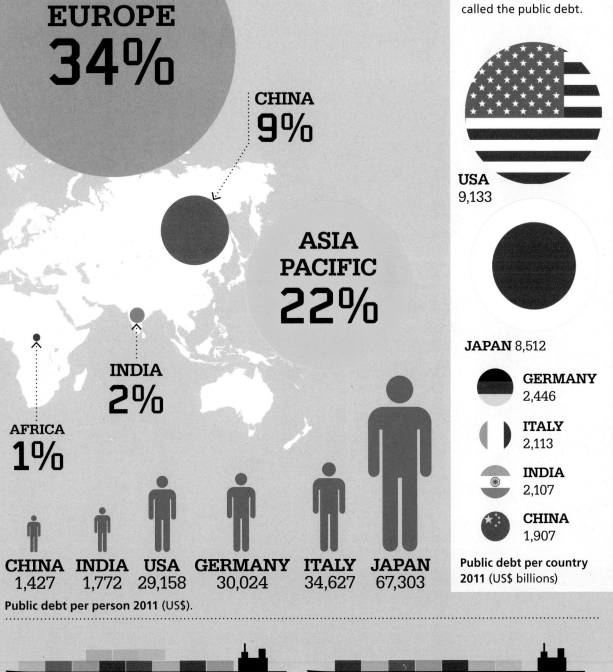

EUROPE
34%

CHINA
9%

ASIA PACIFIC
22%

INDIA
2%

AFRICA
1%

WHO OWES WHAT?

Countries may need to borrow money, for example in order to build hospitals or buy weapons for their armed forces. The money they borrow is called the public debt.

USA 9,133

JAPAN 8,512

GERMANY 2,446

ITALY 2,113

INDIA 2,107

CHINA 1,907

Public debt per country 2011 (US$ billions)

CHINA	INDIA	USA	GERMANY	ITALY	JAPAN
1,427	1,772	29,158	30,024	34,627	67,303

Public debt per person 2011 (US$).

GERMANY 1,198,000,000,000

JAPAN 794,700,000,000

13

GOING GLOBAL

Some of the world's biggest corporations earn more money each year than entire countries. These companies employ thousands, and sometimes millions of people around the globe.

Big earners

The figures in this graphic compare the market value of the world's largest companies. This value is based on the total value of their shares as they are bought and sold at stock exchanges around the world.

APPLE 353,518.1
TECHNOLOGY HARDWARE, SOFTWARE AND EQUIPMENT

EXXON MOBIL 353,135.2
OIL AND GAS PRODUCERS

PETROCHINA 276,473.9
OIL AND GAS PRODUCERS

IBM 208,843.5
SOFTWARE AND COMPUTER SERVICES

MICROSOFT 208,534.9
SOFTWARE AND COMPUTER SERVICES

McDONALD'S
This burger chain sells more than

75

hamburgers every single second and serves about

62,000,000

people every day – that's greater than the population of the UK.

McDONALD'S IS FOUND IN

119

COUNTRIES.

World's largest companies, third quarter 2011 (US$ millions)

GLOBAL EXPOSURE

The figures below show the percentage of the world in which the most widespread companies operate, employ people and sell their goods and services.

XSTRATA
Mining and quarrying 93.2%

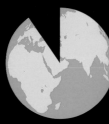

ABB LTD
Engineering Services 90.4%

NOKIA
Electrical and electronic equipment 90.3%

EXXON
Oil and gas production 68%

TOYOTA
Car maker 30.9%

WALMART
LARGEST PRIVATE EMPLOYER IN THE WORLD. IT HAS

8,500

STORES IN 15 COUNTRIES UNDER 55 DIFFERENT NAMES. THESE NAMES INCLUDE WAL-MART, ASDA, SEIYU AND BEST PRICE.

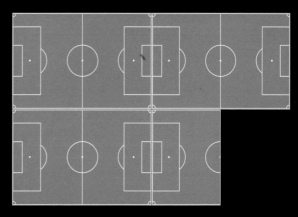

The largest Walmart store is in Albany, New York, USA. It covers 24,154.8 square metres – an area as large as 3.5 football pitches.

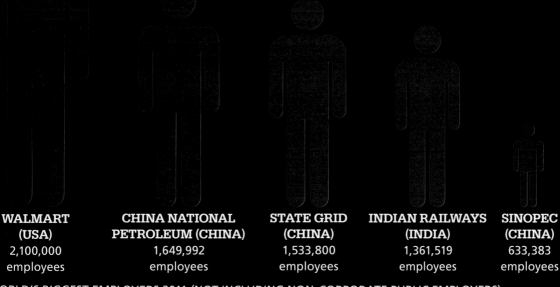

WALMART (USA)	CHINA NATIONAL PETROLEUM (CHINA)	STATE GRID (CHINA)	INDIAN RAILWAYS (INDIA)	SINOPEC (CHINA)
2,100,000 employees	1,649,992 employees	1,533,800 employees	1,361,519 employees	633,383 employees

WORLD'S BIGGEST EMPLOYERS 2011 (NOT INCLUDING NON-CORPORATE PUBLIC EMPLOYERS)

WATER

Without water, life would not be possible. But not everyone has access to safe water, while other people can pour thousands of litres of water down the drain every year.

OF ALL THE WORLD'S WATER...

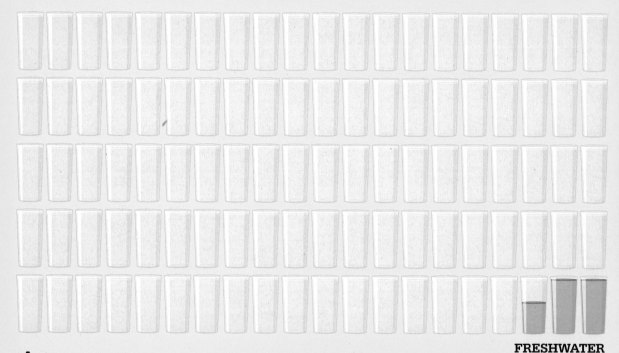

FRESHWATER

2.5%

OF THAT, ONLY

30%

is usable water, the remainder of the freshwater is locked in glaciers.

Access to water

Processing water so that it is safe to drink is expensive and many countries cannot afford to supply their population with safe water. According to the World Health Organisation, 884 million people do not have access to a safe water supply – that is nearly three times the population of the USA.

50 billion bottles of water are bought in the USA every year, creating **US$30 billion** in sales.

According to the UN, this amount of money would be enough to provide everyone on the planet with access to safe water.

WHO USES THE MOST?
water per person per day, in litres.

USA **575**

AUSTRALIA **493**   ITALY **386**   JAPAN **374**

Water usage

A person taking a five-minute shower in a developed country, such as the USA, will use more than 50 litres of water. That is more than a person in a developing country will use in an entire day.

WHO USES THE LEAST?
water per person per day (in litres)

HAITI **15**   RWANDA **15**   UGANDA **15**   MOZAMBIQUE **5**

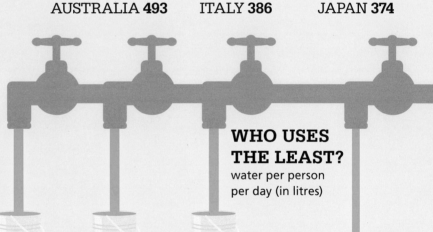

☐ 1 CUP OF COFFEE
140 LITRES

WATER FOOTPRINT

Water is used to produce all the food we eat. But some foods require a lot more processing and so use a lot more water in their production.

1 KG OF CHOCOLATE
24,000 LITRES

1 KG OF BEEF
15,500 LITRES

☐ 1 SLICE OF BREAD
40 LITRES

WHAT A WASTE!

Humans are very wasteful and throw away millions of tonnes of useful food and materials every year. With more careful use, everyone on the planet could be fed with what's discarded.

Where does it go?

The vast amount of material thrown away each year could be recycled and used again. However, most of it is used only once and then discarded in landfill or burned in incinerators.

TRASH TREATMENT AROUND THE WORLD

54%
LANDFILL

24%
RECYCLED

12%
INCINERATED

8%
COMPOSTED

 # 84% COULD BE RECYCLED

NEW YORK CITY PRODUCES 11,000 TONNES OF TRASH A DAY
In our lifetime, 307 million Americans will produce 280 billion cubic metres of rubbish – enough to cover the USA with a layer of trash 2.5 cm deep

Only **20%** of plastic bottles are recycled out of **29.8 billion**. Recycling the other **80%** could earn **US$1.2 billion**, based on a price of 5 cents per bottle

THE CITY OF GUIYU IN CHINA IS THE CENTRE OF A HUGE ELECTRONICS RECYCLING INDUSTRY. EACH YEAR,

5,500

COMPANIES IN THE CITY EMPLOY ABOUT

150,000

PEOPLE TO DISMANTLE COMPUTERS, MOBILE PHONES AND OTHER ELECTRONIC DEVICES.

70%

It takes 70 per cent less energy to make recycled paper than to make paper from raw materials.

1974
900 CALORIES OF FOOD WASTED PER PERSON PER DAY

TODAY
1,400 CALORIES OF FOOD WASTED PER PERSON PER DAY

2,000,000,000

people could be fed with the amount of food the USA throws away each year.

8,300,000

tonnes of food are wasted in the UK every year

30.8% OF ALL FOOD PURCHASED IN THE UK IS THROWN AWAY

2.5 CM

DWINDLING RESOURCES

Humans take resources out of the ground and use them in nearly everything that's manufactured. However, the speed with which we are using these resources mean that many of them will run out very soon.

OIL RESERVES =
1.3 TRILLION
BARRELS

OIL WILL
RUN OUT IN
2053

USA **19,150,000**

CHINA **9,189,000**

JAPAN
4,452,000

INDIA
3,182,000

RUSSIA
2,937,000

ISLAND OF NIUE **40**

OIL – WHO USES THE MOST?
(barrels per day)

Using resources

Everything you use, whether it is a car, a mobile phone or a watch, needs resources to make it. We also use resources to power our homes, factories and work places.

THE RICHEST 20% OF PEOPLE CONSUME 83% OF RESOURCES.

THE POOREST 20% OF PEOPLE CONSUME 1.3% OF RESOURCES.

435

The number of nuclear reactors around the world at the start of 2012.

OTHER RESOURCES –
WHEN WILL THEY GO?
Years remaining of mineral reserves, as of December 2011

COPPER (WIRE, COINS, PLUMBING) 61 YEARS

GOLD (JEWELLERY, DENTAL) 45 YEARS

LEAD (PIPES, BATTERIES) 42 YEARS

TIN (CANS, SOLDER) 40 YEARS

URANIUM (WEAPONS, POWER STATIONS) 59 YEARS

NICKEL (BATTERIES, TURBINE BLADES) 90 YEARS

TANTALUM (MOBILE PHONES, CAMERA LENSES) 116 YEARS

PHOSPHORUS (FERTILISER, ANIMAL FEED) 345 YEARS

COAL PROVIDES NEARLY
30%
OF THE WORLD'S ENERGY NEEDS, INCLUDING POWER AND HEATING

AND IS USED TO GENERATE MORE THAN
40%
OF THE WORLD'S ELECTRICITY.

WORK, REST AND PLAY

As more and more people travel around the world on holiday, the amount of money they bring into other countries can have a huge effect on local economies.

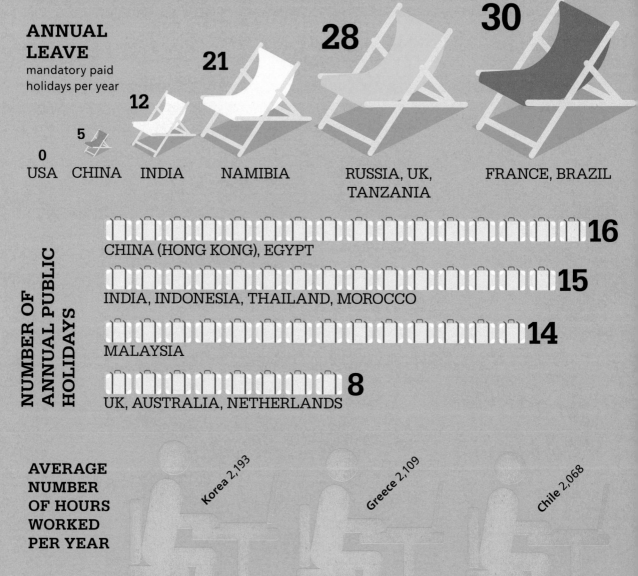

ANNUAL LEAVE
mandatory paid holidays per year

0 USA

5 CHINA

12 INDIA

21 NAMIBIA

28 RUSSIA, UK, TANZANIA

30 FRANCE, BRAZIL

NUMBER OF ANNUAL PUBLIC HOLIDAYS

16 CHINA (HONG KONG), EGYPT

15 INDIA, INDONESIA, THAILAND, MOROCCO

14 MALAYSIA

8 UK, AUSTRALIA, NETHERLANDS

AVERAGE NUMBER OF HOURS WORKED PER YEAR

Korea 2,193

Greece 2,109

Chile 2,068

MOST POPULAR TOURIST COUNTRIES
International tourist arrivals

France 76.8 million

USA 59.7 million

China 55.7 million

Spain 52.7 million

Italy 43.6 million

UK 28.1 million

IN 2010, INCOME FROM INTERNATIONAL TOURISM GREW TO **US$919 BILLION** – THAT IS MORE THAN THE ENTIRE COUNTRY OF TURKEY EARNS IN A YEAR.

TOURISM INCOME
Top three biggest earners from the tourist industry (US$ billions)

USA 103.5

SPAIN 52.5

FRANCE 46.3

LOUVRE
7.5 MILLION

SACRÉ-COUER
8 MILLION

EIFFEL TOWER
6.7 MILLION

CENTRE POMPIDOU
5.1 MILLION

DISNEYLAND PARIS
10.6 MILLION

VERSAILLES
3.45 MILLION

NOTRE DAME
12 MILLION

POPULAR DESTINATIONS IN PARIS
Number of visitors to attractions in the world's most popular tourist city

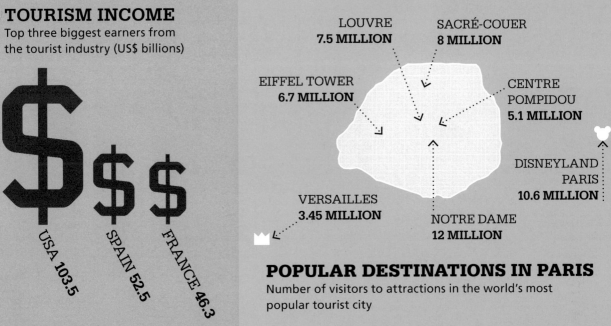

USA 1,778

Japan 1,733

UK 1,647

France 1,554

Netherlands 1,377

STAYING IN TOUCH

The first writing appeared more than 5,000 years ago. Since then, many amazing inventions have greatly changed the way we communicate, allowing us to send messages around the globe in the blink of an eye.

THE INTERNET
The number of people using various languages on the internet.

Languages
There are thought to be up to 7,000 different languages spoken around the world.

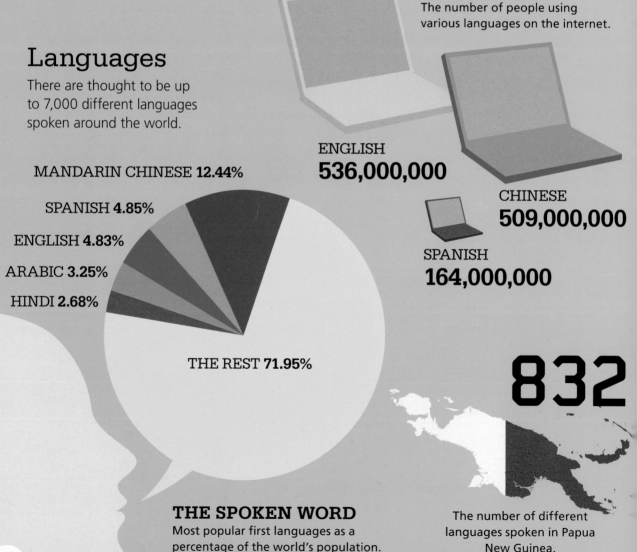

ENGLISH
536,000,000

CHINESE
509,000,000

SPANISH
164,000,000

MANDARIN CHINESE **12.44%**

SPANISH **4.85%**

ENGLISH **4.83%**

ARABIC **3.25%**

HINDI **2.68%**

THE REST **71.95%**

832

THE SPOKEN WORD
Most popular first languages as a percentage of the world's population.

The number of different languages spoken in Papua New Guinea.

TALKING LONG-DISTANCE

Key moments in the history of long-distance communication

HUMAN RUNNER
In 490 BCE, Pheidippides ran 225 km from Athens to Sparta in two days, with news of the Battle of Marathon.

SEMAPHORE TOWERS
The arms on these towers moved to spell out messages. They were used throughout western Europe by Napoleon in the early 19th century.

MORSE CODE
Using dots and dashes, the first morse code signal was sent on 6 January 1838.

PONY EXPRESS
This delivery service reduced message delivery time across the whole of the USA from several weeks to just 10 days.

AIRMAIL
The first official air mail delivery was on 17 August 1859. John Wise piloted a balloon from Lafayette, Indiana, to New York.

TELEPHONE
The first call was made by Alexander Graham Bell on 10 March 1876.

WIRELESS
The first transatlantic radio message was sent in 1901.

MOBILE PHONE
The first call from a mobile phone was made on the 3 April 1973.

In 2010, there were some **5.3 billion** mobile phones in use. The countries with the greatest number were China with **747,000,000** and India with **670,000,000** users.

GOING POSTAL
300,000,000,000
letters are posted each year around the world.

OTHER ITEMS **34%**

LETTERS **66%**

PROPORTION OF ITEMS POSTED EACH YEAR

5,500,000,000
letters are sent internationally.

4,000,000,000
of these are carried by plane.

THE DIGITAL WORLD

The first email was sent in 1971. Today, we type and send nearly 400 times as many emails as we do written letters.

RISE OF THE COMPUTERS
The number of computers has more than doubled since the start of the 21st century.

2000 **140.2 MILLION**

2010 **350.9 MILLION**

EMAIL
There are **3,150,000,000** known email accounts in the world

25% of these are company accounts.

In 2011, there were

2,110,000,000 internet users around the world.

China had **485,000,000** while the US had **245,000,000**.

THE WORLD'S FIRST PROGRAMMABLE, FULLY AUTOMATIC COMPUTING MACHINE WAS THE ZUSE Z3, BUILT IN 1941.

BY THE END OF 2011, THERE WERE

555,000,000 WEBSITES, OF WHICH SOME

300,000,000 HAD BEEN CREATED THAT YEAR ALONE.

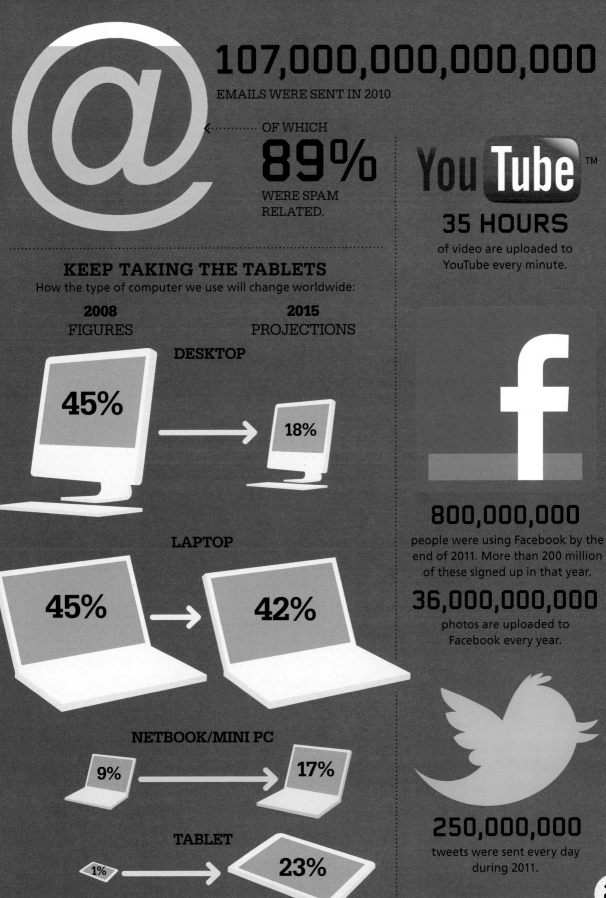

107,000,000,000,000

EMAILS WERE SENT IN 2010

OF WHICH

89%

WERE SPAM
RELATED.

You Tube ™

35 HOURS

of video are uploaded to
YouTube every minute.

KEEP TAKING THE TABLETS

How the type of computer we use will change worldwide:

2008
FIGURES

2015
PROJECTIONS

DESKTOP

45% → 18%

LAPTOP

45% → **42%**

NETBOOK/MINI PC

9% → 17%

TABLET

1% → **23%**

f

800,000,000

people were using Facebook by the
end of 2011. More than 200 million
of these signed up in that year.

36,000,000,000

photos are uploaded to
Facebook every year.

250,000,000

tweets were sent every day
during 2011.

GLOSSARY

air mail
Letters, parcels and other mail that is delivered by air, usually between different countries.

agglomeration
A continuous built-up area, which may be made up of several towns and cities that are joined by suburbs and other urban areas.

composted
When biodegradable materials, such as organic waste, are allowed to rot. This produces compost which can be used to feed crops and gardens.

corporation
A very large company or group of companies.

global exposure
The amount of the world where a company operates and employs people.

debt
The amount of money that is owed by a person, company or even an entire country.

incinerated
When something is destroyed by burning it.

landfill
A large hole in the ground into which waste and rubbish are dumped and then covered over.

mandatory
Something that has to happen. Mandatory holidays are days off that companies have to give their workers.

market value
The total value of a company. This is decided by the value of the company's shares as they are bought and sold at stock markets in various parts of the world.

morse code
An alphabet that uses a system of dots and dashes to represent letters. Morse code signals can be sent using a light or as pulses along electric wires.

population
The people who live in a particular area, such as a country.

population density
The number of people living in a particular area.

public debt
The amount of money owed by a country's government.

public holidays
Holidays that are taken to celebrate occasions that are important to a whole country or a specific group of people.

resources
Materials that can be used to produce goods or energy. These can include natural resources, such as coal, oil and minerals, and human resources, such as the size of a workforce.

semaphore
A system of sending messages using large mechanical arms or flags. The positions of the arms and flags spell out different letters.

shares
A small proportion of a company which can be bought or sold by people or other companies. The total worth of a company's shares decides the company's market value.

stock exchange
A place where company shares and other economic products are bought and sold.

tablet
A small computer device that just has a screen and no keyboard. Instructions are typed directly onto the screen, which is touch-sensitive.

trade
The buying and selling of goods between different peoples, regions and countries.

urban
Relating to towns, cities and other built-up areas.

Websites

MORE INFO:
kids.nationalgeographic.com/kids/places/
Part of the children's section of the National Geographic website. This offers lots of information about different countries.

cyberschoolbus.un.org/
The educational web page for the United Nations. It includes an interactive database with the latest facts and statistics from around the world.

www.cia.gov/kids-page
The children's section of the website for the CIA. It provides links to information about the population and economy of every country on the planet.

MORE GRAPHICS:
www.visualinformation.info
A website that contains a whole host of infographic material on subjects as diverse as natural history, science, sport and computer games.

www.coolinfographics.com
A collection of infographics and data visualisations from other online resources, magazines and newspapers

www.dailyinfographic.com
A comprehensive collection of infographics on an enormous range of topics that is updated every single day!

INDEX

ACKNOWLEDGEMENTS

First published in 2015 by Wayland
Copyright © Wayland 2015

MIX
Paper from
responsible sources
FSC® C104740
www.fsc.org

Wayland, an imprint of
Hachette Children's Group
Part of Hodder & Stoughton
Carmelite House, 50 Victoria Embankment
London EC4Y 0DZ

All rights reserved.

Produced by Tall Tree Ltd
Editor: Jon Richards
Designer: Ed Simkins
Consultant: Dr Vincent Béal

ISBN: 9780750289856

Dewey Number: 301-dc23

Printed in China

An Hachette UK company
www.hachette.co.uk
www.hachettechildrens.co.uk

The website addresses (URLs) included in this
book were valid at the time of going to press.
However, because of the nature of the Internet,
it is possible that some addresses may have
changed, or sites may have changed or closed
down, since publication. While the author and
Publisher regret any inconvenience this may
cause the readers, no responsibility for any such
changes can be accepted by either the author or
the Publisher.